Beautiful Corpus

Beautiful Corpus

Poems of the Body, Mind & Spirit

By

Nancy Brewka-Clark

Cover photograph by Nancy Brewka-Clark
Cover design by Shay Culligan

ISBN: 978-1-950462-82-7

Kelsay Books Inc.

kelsaybooks.com

502 S 1040 E, A119
American Fork, Utah 84003

For Tom

Acknowledgments

I'm grateful to these journals, anthologies and poetry societies for publishing and in several cases awarding prizes to my poems, several of which originally appeared in slightly different form:

New England Poetry Club Amy Lowell Prize: "The Dark Night of Charles Olson"

Helen Schaible International Sonnet Competition: "Whale Watch"

Marblehead Festival of the Arts Writers' World: "Pianist"

Chicagoland Poets & Patrons: "Judicial Branch"

Merton Quarterly, Poetry of the Sacred: "Emily at Her Window"

Better Than Starbucks: "On Admiring a Scythian Cup"

Agape Magazine: "Drowned"

Rhyme On! Loudoun County(VA) Public Library Humor Prize: "To My Dentist"

Two-Countries, Red Hen Press: "My Father's Orchard," "Ukrainian Lesson"

My Mane Memories, Silver Birch Press: "Harum-scarum"

What Remains, Gelles-Cole Literary Enterprises: "Family Plot"

Nurturing Paws, Whispering Angel Press: "New Dog"

Matchbook: Vol. I, Small Fires Press: "Curtains"

Visiting Frost, University of Iowa Press: "Elinor White Frost Speaks"

North American Review: "The Perfume of Hyacinths"

Regrets Only, Little Pear Press: "Broker"

Orchard Press Mysteries: "Counterintelligence"

Hope Whispers, Whispering Angel Press: "Saving Ground"

Period Stories, HerStry: "Picnic"

Beloved on the Earth, Holy Cow! Press: "Poem for My Mother"

Prompt Literary Journal: "Elegy in Five Parts for Tish: Last Seen"

Poetry Quarterly: "Winter Moths"

Flashquake: "Taking Sides"

Book of Remembrance, Cayuse Press: "Manhattan, Dec. 24, 2001"

Riddled with Arrows: "Updike at the P.O."

Sunny Side Down: "Bukowski Theorem"

Literary Medical Messenger: "Tick"

Glass Works, Pudding House : "The Man Who Loved Glass"

Entombed in Verse, FunDead Publications: " Ballad of Jones Very"

Whispers Poetry Journal: "Resonance"

42 Stories, BAM Publishing: "Love in the Fifth Decade"

Pantoums for the 21st Century: "Tiny Odd Museums"

Since this collection is, in essence, an accounting of my life, I have to say that nobody could have been luckier in the lottery of family, friends, education, and marriage. My parents Walter and Annie Brewka, my sister Barbara and her husband James A. Lee, the Wheaton College (MA) faculty and my beloved roommate Betty Clarke Slocombe, two sets of aunts and uncles, the Dicks and the Carpenters, the multitudinous tribe of my in-laws, and above all my wonderful husband Thomas Laing Clark always made me feel like a star even when I was little more than a sputtering sparkler. I also wish to thank Alex Ushakoff of CCI Reprographics for properly formatting the cover photo, which I took in Quebec City. I am infinitely grateful for the recommendations on the back cover penned by Amber Newberry and Laurie Moran of FunDead Publications, Sheryl Normandeau of *Paper Butterfly Flash Fiction,* and the acclaimed poet Martha Collins, whose tenth book was being published just as my first was accepted. And that leads to Karen Kelsay and her publishing house. Because of her interest, I'm finally able to hold in my hands the concrete result of my dreams.

Contents

III. Of Spirits, Animal and Otherwise

I. Of My Own Flesh

Picnic

"One-ninety over one-ten."
The nurse deflates the cuff
with a huff and a puff, taking
measure of the pressure in
being laid bare on an empty
table like an inedible spread.

I'm here because of a problem
with the old picnic basket,
one of the flaps. I've been
a twelve-year-old boy
for nine years. I don't want
to remember the cherry rushes,
the raspberry runs, the libation
to the goddess onto the doormat
of pad. My inner boy doesn't care
that the old swimming hole
has gone dry or that,
down on the playing field,
brittle hay barely covers
the pitcher's mound.

 I receive primary care
from a physician who peeks
in the oven of my antiquated
Vulcan, then calls up a surgeon.
Bacteria bees are swarming in
the slingshot of my crotch,
swelling the gray hive
with toxic honey. Like Pandora,
the surgeon pries open my box.

She's going to pick, not preserve,
my plum. Prick, and the frog-leg
skin twitches. The recipe calls for
a slit in the pie. Lickety-split,
my fat lip is a candle
with an eight-inch wick.
At home, I get an adult
to open the bottle, and chew up
my first white pill, too big
for a boy's throat to swallow.

Harum—scarum

The average human head has 100,000 hairs.
                                —Google Answers

At birth, a hairy head
like a coconut. Black wisps
fall out, brown filaments
grow in their follicles,
the brown of damp earth,
the brown of night soil,
the brown of Victorian studies.

Mummy, hopeful of changing
every hair on this head, snips
with the kitchen scissors until
the uneven jack o'lantern grin
of seven matches an asymmetrical
Chinese fringe meant for thick
skeins of black silk, not one-ply
Eastern European post-war thread.

There's change in the air.
The semi-final solution reeks
in a dish, pearlescent pink.
Curlers snap their tin jaws
onto hanks of saturated hair.
The timer clicks like a bomb.
There's no long-lasting fluff
from this stuff, just brief kinks.

At seventeen, the prom, a chignon,
Joan Baez and Mary of Peter and Paul,
saints to the string-straights, letting
their hair down, letting it all hang out,

leaving it blowin' in the wind that did
somebody good if their hair's long, brown
and ironically doesn't need pressing.

Life unfurls without curls. Every
parting's a sweet sorrow with
a widow's peak. That's the long
and the short of it, some years tucked
behind the ears, others, cropped.

Never bleached, now natural brown's
equivalent to a heavenly crown.
Once it was as common as dirt.
Now it's to dye for.

My Father's Orchard

Apple trees in villages
all speak the same tongue,
a buzz and bumble of hot
pollination at spring's cool
core, when the violets,
past their pale prime,
sink to the ground
like so many
dramatic,
dying
ballerinas.

You left the rolling hills
of western Ukraine
as a boy, alone,
walking some of those
ten thousand miles,
crossing the Atlantic
in the bowels
of a behemoth
to find a hillside in
New Hampshire
that looked
just like home.

So many shadows
on your shoulders,
of men, and women,
and trees
where the breath
of summer inflates

the small, green balloons
of the apples in a party to
surprise you
with their sameness.
You graft, splitting
the branch and fitting it
to a slit in the bark,
binding the cut
until the transplant
stands up for itself.

Pink veins the new buds.
They open
like falling snow.

The shelter is always the same,
cool, dull green
of the heart-like
leaves, and even the voices,
bird and wind,
speaking the language of
apples.

Curtains

Impetus spins
white thread from
the hidden bobbin.
The needle rattles
the platen below it,
sowing a furrow
of stitches.

My father is slaving
over a hot Singer,
making kitchen curtains.
He goes for frills,
ruffled hems to tickle
the sills, three valances
to pucker up
across three rods.

Six pale skirts
fly away from
his hands.

My Father's Daughter

I am a small woman who likes
to build big things. My hands
are the hands of a child,
my skills are those of a
son. I wear my father's gloves,
the leather nearly mummified,
thick fingers stiff as arthritic
flesh, just for the scent of them,
the tallow richness of tung oil,
raw pitch of sawn pine,
blood tang of rusted screws.
A man can't carry a child,
but a woman can carry a board.
She can cut it down to size,
raise it up and make a house,
turn a house into a home, raise
a family. It doesn't depend
on the build, but the will.

White Legs

No one ever had white legs
when my sister and I were
growing up. We sported
the shortest of shorts,
broiling, boiled in baby oil,
until we were well done.

Rare was the day
in July, the sky white hot
like melting pearls,
when we didn't sunbathe
until we bubbled. Boys
with chests as red as
a cardinal's dove into the
sand chasing beach balls and
hot girls. Thousands waded
up to the waist in frigid water,
their radiant skin the bright
pink of bubblegum.

Peeling was unappealing
but it came with the territory.
Paling from beet red to
hen's egg tan with the same
translucent sheen as the
membrane of an egg,
our blistered epidermis
lifted off in sheets.
By the next Sunday we'd
be out there again, bodies
browning like a turkey's,
cooking our goose
in the blazing hot oven
of dumb ultraviolet bliss.

The Perfume of Hyacinths

We were freshwomen,
drunken girls, brain-battered
high on vodka, underage for nothing
but booze. The sheriff's daughter
had a single room
with a sunny windowsill,
and a married boyfriend,
a collegial middle-aged
cheater who parked his truck in the
alley and his boots by her bed.
The window was there, and so was
the opportunity, for growing
spring bulbs or getting him out
and us in after the one a.m. curfew.

It was a confusing time, the mid-Sixties,
after Jackie, but still half Mamie.
We could conceal some things (tampons)
and come clean about others (sex).
We began to think we were guys
without thinking like them,
which was why, when we puked out
our brains in the dorm, often carrying
some stranger's sperm, we came to
in the perfume of hyacinths.

Saving Ground

The last race of the season is going off late.
The heavens have started to spit a cold rain,
staining the churned tan of rutted dirt to
tobacco brown. A few die-hard fans
dot the wide asphalt apron, but the three of us
cling to the rail by the trail where the horses,
riders up, will soon come ambling down.

Taped trumpet notes as familiar as "Taps"
spark a last charge to the betting windows.
My mother Annie, eighty-two, always goes for
odd-ball names like Henbane or Baldski.
Tom, my husband, combs *The Racing Form*.
I, facing surgery in a few days for a first-stage
malignancy of the right breast, scrutinize
the six-point type of dam and sire, trainer,
owner, markings on the jockey's silks,
looking for divine guidance
among these cheapest of fillies and mares
stabled at the bottom of luck's barrel.

I have always been prayerful, clandestinely so,
and never more so than now. My mother
has just paraded before Tom and me in
her kitchen, topless and one-breasted,
as withered and sallow as a store brand of
roasting chicken, seasoned and flecked
with keratoses and liver spots, in a reminder
that she has gone for more than thirty years
without a breast and without mentioning
the loss, even to her own sisters, so I can, too.

It's a double-edged sword, that message,
but I've decided to go her route and play
my cards close to the vest, reasoning that
I won't tell anyone unless I lose my hair
like my sister did from her chemo, after which
she recovered, turned fifty, and got married.

The clubhouse is lit up behind us like some kind
of grand cruise ship, giant glass walls reflecting
the watery scene, damp earth, slanting rain,
black sky, and the white-hot numbers flashing
the relentlessly fluctuating odds on the tote board.
"Muddler," I say. Annie grins. Tom frowns.
"Eleven to one, and good in the mud," I say.
But what I really mean is that I am muddled,
churned up, blaming myself for dying young
(or at least, at forty-seven, not that old)
if I do, which I fervently hope that I don't,
but might, though I don't believe I will.

A bell shrills. Gates clang. "They're off!"
Running in pools of darkness, straining for home,
this handful of horses faces the end of the line,
either too slow or too unpredictable to have won
more than a single race in the past six months.
Muddler, small and brown, breaks fast
but drops to last when her jockey is forced
to swing wide on the far outside.

"Run like the wind," I pray to her, invisible
as the breathing God riffling dark waters.

Muddler gallops into sight in the backstretch,
trailing the pack but edging up on the rail as
she senses there's a way of saving ground.
In the far turn, Muddler's number on the board
flashes to fourth, then third, then second. At the
sixteenth pole Muddler lunges forward and wins.
Her faith in beating the odds will stay with me
under the wire, under the knife, under the gun,
through all the victory laps that I will run.

How Long

Variation on David, Psalm 13

I am counting the days now,
collecting medical test results
like olde-tyme broadsheets
announcing war. They ride
upon electric waves to pummel
my Inbox in a surging tide
pulled by an operating moon
whose round soft eye, winkless,
weepless, lights up the earth.
Projections of unholy terror
spill out onto the screen
in words, not moving pictures.
Who will fix this bloody reel,
stop the verbal carnage in its
tracks? If ignorance is peace,
I choose war. If war is death,
I choose heaven for this hell.

Resonance

I lie like an astronaut
in the capsule exploring
my own inner space.
My body's a hidden landscape,
blood ocean, bone mountain,
magnetic minerals, guts.
I have been terrified of
being terrified, but now,
lying here in this crackling
sarcophagus without having
sacrificed my own living
organs to an oncological
augury, I am grateful.
I am thankful for cool air,
the softness of the pad
beneath my strapped ankles
and gowned flesh. As some
delicate distant music plays,
I have a vision of morning glories
on their strong green vines
budding all about me,
lowering and lifting their
faces of heavenly blue tissue,
and my heart names each one,
holding it as a prayer until
the next familiar face comes
into bloom. In this way I
survive my inward journey
and surprise myself by being
just slightly sorry to be
released before I can bless
every soul in this glorious world.

To My Dentist

How joyful did I feel when in that chair
I lay my head, my mouth pried open wide,
benumbed and prepped for your assessing stare,
assistant's hookah gurgling at my side
to suction off saliva lest I drown
ere last old tooth to youth has been restored
like deposed monarch fitted with a crown
that, uninsured, takes all I can afford.
Lo, all these many years I've paid the cost
when X-rays showed the shadows of decay.
Despite the fact I've always brushed and flossed
Each checkup meant a check was on its way.
Now each tooth's a pearl without a filling.
I'm so done with drilling, billing. Thrilling!

Family Plot

Buying a coffin's easier than it sounds.
After all, it isn't as if we have to live with it.
The mortician's young enough to be our son.
Our ties go deep. His grandfather buried
our grandparents. His father buried our dad.
Somber at the start of the negotiations,
he eventually sees we're stable, not going
to go to pieces, not going to do much
but sit there dry-eyed, two married sisters
over fifty, over any vestigial fear
of being orphaned. Eventually the three of us
descend into the showroom where he's parked
a lot of caskets bumper to bumper. He steers
the two of us to a Rolls Royce, snow white
with an enameled plaque of violets
bunched around a calligraphic "Mother"
on the lid. We admire the quilted satin,
brass handrails, bulletproof liner,
but buy a modest Ford the sheen
and tint of a mourning dove. Above ground,
starting to fill out the paperwork, he says,
"Gosh, ladies, I think I left the light on
down there. Do me a favor and shut it off?
The switch is at the bottom of the stairs."
When only one of us moves to stand up,
he shakes his head. "Don't go alone."
Back down we go, quietly sharing a laugh.
Does he really think empty coffins
would scare us to death? Then it dawns on us
what he hopes we'll do: pick out another two.

Broker

He blows in begging on a March blizzard,
the original fair-haired boy who poisoned himself
with bad alchemy, a strung-out harbinger of
spring groaning up the driveway in his
broken-down Chevy to knock at the door and
sell himself once more with a sly humility.
He's checked himself out of the private asylum
where a born-again client had insisted on footing
the bills to raise him from the wreckage of his
Wall Street minerals firm, gold stock blown to
angel dust. When I tell him my mother, his aunt,
had died and been buried back in February,
he sits, candy belly bulging, staring that ward stare.

Outside, wearing a loose, brownish kimono—
God knows what institutional laundry spawned it—
and boat shoes with rawhide laces untied, his thighs
fat as a jolly friar's or a murderous Henry the Eighth's,
he smokes unfiltered Camels behind the wheel,
radio on and door open while we boil his clothes.
At night, the stairs creak. Our whole bodies cock
for the surreptitious slide of the knife drawer, lunatic
rummage among mouse turds and twist-ties.
The bathroom door opens and closes, opens again.
We don't grow used to this, even though it proves
time after time after time after time that he hasn't
come to kill us but to favor us with his need.

It snows. It snows again, harder. Outside, he shifts
behind the wheel and smoke pours out into the world
from his mouth like a terrible idea. In his fantasy,
he's still rich, owns us all, owns the world, the roads,

the churches, the towers, the mines and the caves
where, like Ali Baba, he first met the thieves. At night,
the phone calls monitor the madness of a man who
won't work if he can't steal by peddling nothing real.

On his birthday, we have a cake, and a fight.
There's no money here, no sanctity, no solicitude,
only grief like a hangover, rage for the end of things.

Poem for My Mother

Not having her in the world
is the strangest thing. Right now,
a winter wind is blowing sunlight
against the treetops, smashing it
into a million atoms of joy.

She herself found joy in every
lucent leaf, each kiss of transient
breeze against the cheek of
the earth. She watched the short,
sweet month of February with its
red hearts, lace and lengthening
light, the promissory note
of spring, come due with
interest every year, never jaded,
always mailing a card with
X's and O's to her middle-aged
daughters. When she died we said
it was time, at eighty-eight, no
broken hearts here, she had a full
life, she was ailing, she was failing.

But in this light, with the snow
dripping off the roof and the branches
tossing, this light like a voice calling to
the sleeping bulbs, the burrowing
roots, this breath of fresh wind with
its sting and its kiss, as much as I
honor the spirit, I ache to touch flesh.

Drowned

So many decades drinking to your health
has wasted you and led you to destroy
a tie once prized, accounting for a wealth
of wrenching memories. You can't enjoy
the lacerating of two hearts, yours, mine,
with every jaundiced word or caustic sneer,
since even the most calculated line
is often punctuated with a tear.
The accusations fly. They flay me, ill
from wondering if I indeed had said
the things you say I did, as if my will
had withered like cut flowers for the dead.
A capsized wreck, our freighted friendship sinks
beneath a mindless sea of countless drinks.

Links

My family has a
history of succulents,
three tough old sister
Christmas cactuses,
already mature
in 1958 when my mother
buried her mother,
and a myriad of
offshoots, some in
their own pots, others
perpetually rooting
in tepid water.

As in every family,
some age more gracefully
than others. Of the three,
one wets the rug. Another
displays yellow pillows
of shriveled flesh.
The third's a jade
fountain, each billow
tipped with the tiniest
milk tooth of a bud.

On the anniversary
of my own mother's death,
I tend my antiquarian indoor
garden as usual, a quart
of tap water for each sister,
less for the smaller plants.
I mist with a plastic bottle

the mystical color of a
deep-mined amethyst.
Like Prince Charles, who
once upon a time was ridiculed
for talking to his plants,
I breathe out a prayer composed
of carbon dioxide and my own
earthly hopes.

Later that evening, I hear a
hiss from beneath the bench
on which they sit.
Smoke curls up
in a chemical stench.
I rush over in time to see
the old extension cord
burst into sparks.
Water glistens on the joined
plugs. One yellow iris
of a flame shoots up.

As I crush it beneath
my foot, an absurd thought
strikes me: I'm having
a Merton moment, but
hopefully not my last.
In one searing second,
Father Thomas, Trappist
priest and popular poet
whose gentle voice
paradoxically rang strong

in a clamorous world,
died stepping in
just a little bit of water
spilled in a bedroom
in steamy Bangkok,
an old electric fan
cranking death
in his face like a
vengeful angel.
His sole was bare,
mine protected by a
rubber running shoe
made in China.
How quickly I had stepped
toward my own mortality,
heedless of the
hidden current pulsing,
random, mercurial,
protean, holy, shocking.

Love in the Fifth Decade

With frequency
I deliver a speech
citing my own
short fuse and the
need for absolute
obedience.
I stagger around
pointing to my
leaky heart and swear
I'll be gone before him.
Then we have
a good laugh and eat
some pineapple.

Kissing Sonnet

I celebrate the joy of loving you,
of having you, my partner, by my side
so I can share my life, as lovers do,
with virtually nothing left to hide.
I wake up in the middle of the night,
jolted into replaying all my fears
until you kiss me and they all take flight
into the darkness of the bygone years.
Lying spooned together drifting into sleep,
I feel our heartbeats synchronize as one.
Our breathing slows in rhythm, calm and deep.
Sweet trust will quell what fear had once begun.
If I could live forever, I'd wish this:
that I'd awaken each day to your kiss.

II. Of Like Minds

Elinor White Frost Speaks

I didn't think there was room in the world for yet
another poet, which is why I took the leather pamphlet
you handed me through a door I didn't even wish to open,
thumbed through, and turned away from you.

I couldn't think of a use in the world for a man who wrote
about butterflies, not unless he was dissecting one to
contribute to science. I had thought you smarter than that,
Dartmouth-bound with your bread family-buttered.

New Hampshire, Massachusetts, Vermont,
all cold places, that's what I learned from you,
all about cold places, England, too. Even in August,
the unmowed hay looked like drifting snow.

My politics: I ate off your words, hating my own
handouts. I had been entitled once, to be read like an
open book, but somewhere along the line, I shut
that trap. My duty was to love you cover to cover.

Updike at the P.O.

All of Beverly Farms, Massachusetts,
bears the stamp of exclusivity
except for the post office, democratic
in its service, uniform in uniforms,
faces of the haunting Wanted on the walls.
When John Updike mailed a manuscript
in front of me on an icy day in the 1980s,
behind the narrow counter stood the clerk,
a surly fellow, burly, sourly affixing
a colorful collage of stamps to his manila
as he would to mine. Our manuscripts
were even bound for the same place,
The New Yorker. But my submission
was stuffed with a SASE, that humble
two-way traveler puffed with hope going,
still fat yet somehow deflated coming back.
Updike's left no room for rejection.
His ochre envelope, addressed with an
authoritative hand in inky copperplate,
had already been licked shut elsewhere
and taped with cellophane across the flap.

Bukowski Theorem

Sometimes you have to
read other poets for a while,
to get yourself steady.
Shaky business, this is,
not a business at all unless
by sticking your nose
into everyone else's
business you can get
some kind of charge
out of a ripped ticket,
canceled flight,
someone else's hatred
on the tongue
like a wasp,
can't swallow it,
can't spit it out
and let it buzz away,
not your tongue anyway,
not your business,
nobody's business,
this string of
blue-collar thoughts,
lines hanging out there
for everyone to see,
which is no skin off
your nose if it
isn't your business.
Aw, go cry in your beer.

Ukrainian Lesson

What do I bring to the table?
A shoebox found in the back
of a closet with letters opened
after the war—every
war's cold there—written in
lavender ink. What news, now history,
do they carry of aunts, uncles, cousins,
the family my father never saw again?
Who knows, until the code's cracked.

"Consider what is big, *bolshoi,*
In thick Cyrillic syllables.
We must learn to slip the
glottal bolts and barricades."

In the alphabet, one character
bellies up to consonants complex
as cathedrals. The Trappist monk
of tongues, the squat configuration
is a *makisnyak,* seen but not heard
in almost every word.

"The tongue must suck against the teeth
like a hungry peasant's, then double back
like a soldier camouflaging tracks in snow.
Da svidanya means good day, it is a farewell."

Da svidanya, my dear *makisnyak,*
Friar Fatso, *bolshoi* comrade
quiet as a cabbage. This purple prose
is more a maze than a Czarist bibelot
in its construction. I'll keep my words
by Webster, and just read between the lines.

The Man Who Loved Glass

Henry Davis Sleeper, 1878-1934

Harry Sleeper was born in Boston, died in Boston,
and summered on Cape Ann to the north, in a
seaside mansion called Beauport. Built over three
decades, the house boasted forty rooms, no two
alike, from early American to European, French
in particular. Harry himself was particular, not to
mention peculiar, many would say. Suffering
problems of the blood and the heart all his life,
bachelor esthete with a penchant for wearing ecru,
he turned to collecting glass of all colors and uses.
Some rare, some of it five-and-dime (by chance
the daughter of F. W. Woolworth bought the place
after he died and cherished every piece), all of it's
stunning in sunlight or back-lit against frosted panes,
hand-blown, molded, pinched, stoppered and cut,
fingerbowls, candlesticks, pitchers and honey pots,
saucers and ewers and bottles and syrup jars,
beacons of cobalt and amethyst, amber and ruby,
emerald, garnet, sapphire, opal, some clear as a tear,
intaglio, acid-etched, sketched with engraving tools,
curliqued, monogrammed, lace-edged and footed.
Basalt bottles, tipsy tumblers, primitive pontils,
grass-green bull's-eye panes all honor the colonies.
He framed pastel Sandwich glass from Cape Cod
in an ancient recycled arched window. Sills hold
fuchsia-swirled witches' balls, once hung over a
Puritan doorway to lure mischievous spirits up
into their glistening orbs. Upstairs and downstairs
and in every chamber, the magical glass in the
Sleeper collection not only shines but enlightens.

Ballad of Jones Very

Mystic, Poet, Madman 1813-1880

Sing a sad song if you must,
for poor Jones Very, turned to dust.
Strange his birth, and hard his life,
filled with madness, loss, and strife.
Yet briefly did his star arise
to bring him honor in men's eyes.
Born in an inauspicious year
to two first cousins, it was here
in Salem where he learned to write.

A child too shy, a boy too bright
to bear the shame of parents unwed,
their offspring lying six to a bed,
his seaman father took him at ten
to Russia, then sailed out again
to die in New Orleans. Young Jones
came home a wraith of skin and bones.
"Man of the family," his mother said,
"You'll have to keep us clothed and fed."

By night he studied Latin, Greek.
By day he taught. His life looked bleak.
When he was twenty, fortune struck,
the only time he had good luck.
An uncle seeing him strive for knowledge
paid his fees to Harvard College.
The School of Divinity came next,
where he pondered sacred text
until the word of God flared bright
through every searing, tortured night.
His soul ablaze, he stayed to teach,

but lessons turned to ways to preach
the Second Coming: he was the one
that God had chosen as his son.
Fired, Jones Very came back home,
baptizing people with aplomb
'til his own pastor cried, "Insane!"
and promptly sent him to McLean
Asylum. Jones, upon release
returned to Salem, seeking
peace of mind. His friends,
including Hawthorne, made amends,
recognizing work transcending
any mundane, mortal ending.

Spectral, hollow-cheeked and sad,
Very was no longer mad.
He lived another forty years
but, genius fled, he kept aloof
from any pilgrim seeking proof
that Jones had touched the face of God
when all he'd been was very odd.

The Dark Night of Charles Olson (1910-1970)

Gloucester, Massachusetts, November, 1968

At two in the morning a poet six-foot-eight casts a long shadow,
pen-named MAXIMUS passing from streetlight to the water,
walking the crescent of Pavilion Beach with both hands
buried in satin—it lines the pockets of his outsized coat—
staring toward the lighthouse on Ten Pound Island
where the fishing boats will plow past into the raw dawn.

Gulls don't follow the out-bound boats at dawn,
but wait like ladies' ghosts for tea time to shadow
the catch coming in around the scruffy little island,
dipping like white gloves into oily water.
Sometimes a spot of bloody offal makes a corsage on a coat
of greenish gear grease dumped by deckhands.

After his bad augury—fishing expedition—it's out of his hands,
but it doesn't seem that way, not here, waiting for dawn
to crack that black rim into full morning. He shivers in a coat
heavy as grief, his gut churning at all the clichés: to be a shadow
of his former self, a shade… but it's all writ in water:
anything can change, a man, a poem, a cell, an island.

He'd come to Gloucester like Prospero, washed up on an island
to wreak magic out of Dogtown's ancient deeds. In his hands
the prosaic—cellar holes of houses built, burnt, moved by water,
arcane principles at work in the myths of possession—led to the
dawn of a new civilization: his Oceana. (Finding COURAGE in
the shadow of Babson's runic boulder, he'd saved a pebble
in the pocket of his coat.)

In the dark, he can just make out the old paint factory: one coat
of Tarr & Wonson copper paint kept off the barnacles. The island
and Rocky Neck, they've been painted too, in sunlight and in
shadow by Lane and Prendergast, Homer (sighted Winslow) and
Hassam, dab hands at prettifying what nature made gloriously,
sunset, storm, dawn, though even he had never bested (blind
Greek) Homer's "wine-dark water."

Words from Genesis float into his head like wreckage on water:
he's read too many myths to see God's face in the mirror. His coat
catches a wave and for an instant, he wonders if it would dawn
on anyone that he'd meant to go like this, to the island,
wading Woolf-like to the lighthouse. But it's cold, and his hands
shake and his bones ache and he has no wish to die, not in her
shadow.

In the shadow of the abandoned Birdseye plant, he grabs his coat
and wrings water from the slapping hem. He stops at the traffic
island, turns to see the hands of the City Hall clock, then faces
down the dawn.

*(Note on the sestina format: six stanzas of six lines each repeat the initial six end
words in a specific order. The last three lines repeat all six words. Some of the
lines here are too long to fit on the page, so to maintain the format, their end
words have been dropped to a separate line.)*

Special

*By 1958 she was married to poet and Harvard instructor
Ted Hughes and working as a clerk in Boston.*
                                    —Sylvia Plath biography

The single peach, skin ruddy
as an alcoholic's flush, lies heavy
in her hand. Its dense flesh curves
around a stone as red as the strange,
far star of Mars, the hidden kernel
pitted with canals like runes carved
on a cleric's amulet of cinnabar.
"Special Today," the sign reads,
"Peaches 20 Cents a Pound." Instead
of jam or shortcake, she thinks of
Ezra, bruised from the pounding
of politics gone rotten, his cantos,
like her quatrains, sprung from a
spell in the pit of the madman's cell.
In the scale, the peach sits like
a baby in its bath, the metal sides
angled up to protect it from a fall.
She adds another and the whole pan
jiggles, the needle going haywire
like an Applause-O-Meter they use
on the greedy TV game shows she
catches from the corner of her eye
in the windows of the Lechmere store
as she rides to Cambridge on the T.
Words jangling through her head like
tokens tumbling, she squeezes onto the
laden train to hang by a strap above the
Charles. Her peaches fill the clumsy,
squealing car with siren scent. She rocks
her way to Ted inside the hallowed square
as the working world turns crimson.

54

Counterintelligence

Burns' wee mousie, Aesop's ant,
some folks love them, but I can't.
Living with me, neither for me
nor against me, they don't see
me. I am too big to comprehend,
god not of beginning but of end.
The wedge of poison's pie
sports a brown and yellow crust. I
tear off the lid. I hide the box.
Adipose mouse, it knocks
my beloved mug over, draining
in the dish rack. Braining
it's impossible. Pellets scatter.
Which has the better gray matter?

May

In the 60s, at college, I met quite a few poets.
Sometimes I entered a poetry contest and won.
Once the two events meshed when I was invited
to read at the Harvard Faculty Club. L.E. Sissman,
Ed to his advertising clients, forty and fatally
afflicted with Hodgkin's, was being awarded the
New England Poetry Club Golden Rose Award
for his book of lyric elegies *Dying: An Introduction*.
I was getting one of their budding writer's prizes
for a poem about a frog. I traveled to Cambridge
from Manchester, N.H. by Trailways bus, twenty
and smoking Kools. It was late May, foggy,
rainy, wet, and the square had a literary air about it,
reeking of tweed and sex. In the unequipped restroom,
I got my period. Lightning knocked the power out
just as I got up to read my poem. Mrs. Sissman was
stunning in premature black. I wore a short sheath
with a ruff like a queen's or a frog's. My shoes were
high-heeled sling-backs and my slim legs were tan.
All of this struck me as fodder. As I said, I was twenty.

Two decades later, my mother-in-law's best friend,
a retired fourth grade teacher, unmarried but in
a Boston marriage, genteelly if naively defined
as when females are joined at the mind and not the hip,
and enriched by an inheritance garnered from real estate
in Harvard Square, took an interest in my writing,
wondering why I wasn't. I told her I'd won prizes,
but I couldn't remember the names of any judges
until I came up with May Sarton, a New Hampshire
poet who wrote with unabashed affection about her love

of women. Dorothy lit up. She sent me all May's books with
little notes of encouragement. I saw myself writing poems
about grief and granite, weaving tales like blue tapestries out of
words of love for my native home's hills, but didn't.

After Dorothy and just about every poet I'd read in my
college days was dead, I found the judge's letter.
It wasn't May Sarton at all, but Swenson,
May Swenson, no more New England than the Great Salt Lake.
I should have calculated better, cultivated a relationship
or at least a contact, but I never thought of that.
To take the prize but miss the point—what an inverse talent.
Over the years and in my mind, I invented the phrase
"living up to my *poetential*" but never found a way
to use it, although someday I may still write a poem about it.

Pianist

Notes need judicious sowing,
as does seed. The left hand
plants the dark, rich loam of bass.
A finger slips; it rankles
like a weed. The right hand's work
is fine as Queen Anne's lace.

The hands are spread like birds' wings.
Fingers tug and pluck a chord
like beak at stubborn worm,
then flitter up the keyboard.
Pedal down, one deep note lingers
like fled thunder in a summer's
played-out storm.

Emily at Her Window

Decoration Day, Amherst, MA, May 30, 1870

In white, I am my mind's bride, husbanding
each page. I drink in all colors, spectral
though I am—a sight—writing by my window.
My mother-of-pearl fingers sieve the light.
Men—I've read of them—weigh dark
upon the heart. My soul flies up, though, at
the sight of them, down there where the walls
of lilacs, lavender and white, expire. I am lunar,
they are suns, too bright by far to fit
the silken sheath of my desire. My soul resides
by God's design in the cloister of my bones.

Creation Song

Babies born in autumn—not in summer
when the silver breeze runs like a brush
through the meadow's mane of golden grass
and berries redden the bramble, but in fall
when acorns splatter the rooftops like rain—
tend to be bookish, and write too many poems.

There's no rhyme or reason to it, loving poems
enough to write them in the unschooled summer.
The words come tumbling fast, like rain
as it wets the acorns overhead with its silver brush,
the poet stumbling for cover as the crystal droplets fall
while fumbling for a line that rhymes with grass.

Unlike lions stalking prey through stone and grass,
poets pass on herds of words to flesh out poems
that limp along like wounded antelope about to fall
down bleeding in the baleful glare of summer,
seeking something fresher than a hackneyed brush
with death to write about with tears that fall like rain.

While not averse to every verse that might contain rain,
the poet born in autumn sees the days like blades of grass
that no longer need rain. The coming brush
with death won't strike at the root but might wither poems
praising in flowery phrases the last buds of summer.
In nature, after all, it's unnatural to give birth in the fall.

In a short while the grass will freeze and the snow will fall,
And the wind will lash spume from the water like rain.
It takes a light spirit to brighten things up, to conjure
summer when crystal droplets spill onto the green grass
like clear thoughts in luminous poems rendered
with words instead of a dripping wet brush.

Some might say the sharper the image the finer the brush.
Summer may be rendered as a pearly blur. That's not true of fall.
Fall's colors are leonine, red tongues of flame in golden poems
sifting down in a strangely festive rain
to light on the frozen grass.
Beneath the leaves, the living roots dream of summer.

Summer writes its own ending, rushing toward fall
 in August when stirring leaves brush the roof like rain
and the grass grows unruly like the mane of a lion, or poems.

Boston Bluestocking

Elizabeth Peabody, matronly, virginal,
abolitionist, feminist, always original,
Henry James' Birdseye and penniless Brahmin,
opened a bookstore a block from the Common.
Her West Street emporium, never a boring one,
transcended the mundane to feature a roster
of intellects curious, some of them spurious,
not that she minded. This attitude cost her.
Her heart throbbed for Hawthorne, he married
her sister, finding Sophia less meddlesome, then
Dial-ing her life away, published him anyway,
proper Bostonian living alone. She found men
didn't suit her needs. She, like the Pleiades,
shone through her sisters, her books and her pen.

Why Poetry

Poetry comes out,
like the best china,
when there's
a special occasion.
It's polished, like the
heirloom flatware,
until you can see
yourself in it.

III. Of Spirits, Animal and Otherwise

Tick

You, innocent target
with the big dirt ball
in your arms,
do you know
you're cradling
a tiny assassin?
In the stalks
of the windflower,
aka, Japanese anemone—
it'll look like a bush of
sliced boiled eggs
in October when
the huge leaves
hang gray but the
long stalks are still
swinging their white buds
like bunched baby fists—
an insect the size of
a poppy seed but not
anywhere near as benign
is clocking in. Sometime
in the next few days
a pink patch will appear
on your arm. It'll itch.
You'll treat it.
It won't go away.
In a week you'll sweat
like the toilet tank
in August. You'll be
in a fever to garden,
digging and weeding,
planting and panting.
You'll roll up your sleeve:
bull's eye.

New Dog

What has four paws and a heart
as big as the full moon?
Now it's a fuzz ball, all tumbles
and tangled legs, crazed by a
shoelace.
Now it's a gangly goose of a pup,
sliding on floorboards like a puck.

The love is unconditional,
warm as flesh,
strong as bone,
saying with every breath,
"Home."

Judicial Branch

A dozen basalt magistrates croak laws
in raucous caucus from the ancient oak.
Their voices raised in righteously just caws
with no appeal is likely to provoke
black thoughts from those awakened by the din
at dawn, when birdsong's tentative and hushed.
Without a qualm, this conclave must begin
by cross-examining the freshly crushed,
night's roadkill sentenced not by "Caw!" but car.
Death penalty being paid, squirrel corpus lies
below the creaking branch upon the tar,
being feasted on by greedy onyx eyes
before the flock swoops down to peck its fill
with lawyerly dispatch of dreaded bill.

Taking Sides

A helmet in a war zone,
the turtle straddles
the yellow line,
the narrow safe center
of the dangerous world
into which it has scrabbled,
amphibious detail invading
from the pond's black depths
the flat black surface
of impenetrable tar.

Submersion is impossible
no matter how it wills itself
to disappear beneath
the mapped globe
of its own back.

Where could it possibly
be going?

As my mother used to say
when a squirrel dashed out
right in front of
the screaming tires,
"Why doesn't it stay
where it belongs?"
A nation of naturally
enfranchised creatures
uncivilly disobedient
 to the law of
who must go where when,

none of them have
figured out yet
that their world is
not only shrinking,
it's considered by most of
the ruthlessly territorial
species thundering by
to be expendable.

Tree huggers, we pull over,
hearts bleeding.
I grab a cardboard box
from the trunk of the car,
step out and wave it at
the maniac barreling at me
in her late-model tank.
She doesn't even swerve.
The under-carriage passes
right over the turtle,
whose head lifts.

The next car stops,
and then another.
Before I can airlift it,
the turtle hares off
much faster than legend says,
zigzagging back under
the weedy chain-link fence
where I swear I see it panting.
Do I lock eyes with it?

I don't know, I don't really
think so, and yet somehow
I read in the challenge of
the elevated head,
elongated neck bright
with racing stripes,
the blind confidence of
the young foot soldier,
the grunt,
who thinks that once
I have been appeased
by his appearance
of cowardice,
or wisdom,
he will finally be able
to slip back
toward enemy lines,
invade the soft shoulder
lying so nearby and crawl
into the asphalt world
he's just dying to conquer.

The Heart of the Matter

When the heart rattles the bars of its cage,
ape its rage.

When the heart spreads its wings with a jubilant shriek,
shut its beak.

Tell it to learn from the mole, from the bruin,
hibernating alone is the safeguard from ruin.

When it scrabbles in corners squeaking its need,
give it a negative on which to feed.

Some hearts don't know no and there's no way to teach
the ignorant organ to practice, then preach
the cure for its bliss.
Tell it this:
yes.

Whale Watch

Soft wash of silvered sea and pearly sky
suspends the boats like petals on a pond.
The vapor of the whales' breath is a sigh
that signals life which is so far beyond
our human comprehension that we clap
like circus seals who trumpet out a tune
by rote, no note, no scale between the gap
of blowing and our cheering. Awed, we soon
delight in a fandango of two whales,
a barcarole of boulder backs and fins.
We see the broken hearts of their splayed tails
but humor's in their antics, playful twins.
From deep beneath the boat, they rise. We stare.
A mutual amusement fills in the air.

Land Claim

The chair, the lake,
the black-brush firs,
khaki shorts,
blue cotton shirt
open at the neck,
golden filaments
of hair on tanned skin:
the family album
opens every August
to the same spot.

Gin's in the glass,
or perhaps a beer,
while the earth
swallows the sky
and the sun sets,
resting first on
the upraised arms
of the birches
before going down
in flames.

Everything's blue now.
The skunks grub
with damp paws
through leaves
tannin-stained
like old moccasins
beaded with
pinpricks of mold.
The air in the cabin
cools to comfort.
The moon is slivered
by branches.

Bears, wolves,
bobcats,
antlered bucks
of caribou and elk,
shaking their
cartoon personas,
haunt the painted
cave of dreams.
Flint scratches
cut deep, animated,
they come
hunting the man
who chopped
the tree
and scorched
the ring in the
compromised earth.

On Admiring a Scythian Cup

The stag god on his golden knees looks up,
eternally positioned for the ax.
A hunt in progress swirls around the cup.
A lion licks its chops as it attacks.
In ancient Russia's unearthed cache the skill
of ageless artistry speaks to the heart,
revealing both the urge to praise and kill
embodied in religion and its art,
the bridle plate, the pectoral, the sword,
the burnished mirror flashing in the sun,
the savage song but reverent whispered word
appeasement for the deed which must be done.
The gods die daily, man but once, yet he
creates to prove his own divinity.

Thought for the Day

Six days into January, pixels of rain
pelt the snowman windsock, jingling
his bells. The inspirational calendar
says it's Epiphany, but a line of type
celebrates a different revelation from
the traditional tale of three wise men
divining a savior under a startling star.

"Florence Nightingale carried
a pet owl in her pocket."

Was this in Crimea? Did she pass
from crushed body to body on the
terrible battlefield with a lantern in
one hand, the other hand fondling a
contraband owl? How big was this
pocket? How small was this owl?
Did it get out much? Talk about owl
heaven, carrion as far as the eye can
see, that is, if she allowed it to see.
Perhaps, like an English falcon,
the owl was hooded but at hand if
the soldiers and their nurse were
plagued with mice as well as lice.

Internet research reveals that the owl's
name was Athena; she saved it from
boys who were tormenting it,
in Greece, in the early 1850s.
She also heard angels in birdsong,
rescued a tortoise named Jimmy,
and lived to be ninety—
the day's Web epiphany.

Hawk Strike

In the gray cave of afternoon,
birds bounce at the pine's foot.
The red squirrel is riding the feeder.
His papal beneficence scatters
largesse: seeds of sunflowers,
black/brown like the pecking birds,
and sunny kernels of corn. Millet,
barley, grains from the western
plains lie sown in the snow.

Little god, how he swings,
clinging to the pine box until
he loses purchase and flies back
to the crackelure of the trunk.

The strike is quick: one minute
he's lord of the flying, the next
crazily running for cover, making
an auburn streak across the
blue snow. I see it all from the
living room, the hawk's descent,
plunging like Lucifer, mottled wings
wide, to pluck the littler god
from the earth. High he raises him,
higher still, while I give chase,
hatless, coatless, gloveless,
oddly legless, pitching snowballs.

There, in the naked tree, the
squirrel's tail hangs down like the
flag of a defeated nation seized
in an endless battle to rule the
earth, the sky, the seeds of life.

Winter Moths

The night before my aunt's funeral—
last of my mother's tribe, youngest
sister dead at the age of eighty-five after
a fall in rehab, over backward with a split
in her scalp and a new hip—
the Christmas air swarmed with pale moths,
synchronized wings fanning the icy grit
on the road low down in the headlights,
opening and closing like white kisses
from a dead woman's mouth.

Pressed like pairs of palms against the sliding
glass door, some of them had black designs
up at the body's join to the pearly wing, wooly
like the cape of old man death himself,
shaking loose from the mothball smell
of his dusky cloak to spatter the night
with white arcs of shimmering, shivering
dance. Others folded like penitent's hands,
prayerful, steepled to heaven.

In the old white church on the cold white hill,
the latte-colored coffin sat in a fiery ring of roses,
red roses pretending to be alive on their easels.
The coffin had a short ride in a long hearse
to the family plot, where I stood on my
mother and father next to the green baize cloth
over the hole. On Memorial Day,
I'll dig down a little, trowel scraping up roots,
to plant geraniums, petals red as roses, or white
like the wings of a creature enamored of light.

Manhattan, December 24, 2001

See the anxious salesmen through the
golden windows of the stores on Madison.
Luxury goods. What are they?
Linens. Chocolates. Sapphire studs.
And essentials?
Confidence,
fortitude,
& faith.

On the subway to lower Manhattan,
all is calm, all is bright. Few bags,
No boxes. Just a lemon-yellow light
flickering to black
& back.

Canal Street: hot dogs frying next to
kebabs, cheap watch knock-offs, glittery
scarves, chains of dripping silver,
& very little litter.

Down Broadway, the barricades
begin. Something's chewing up the
ground down there, mechanical
& monstrous.

There is no way to zero in.

Block to block the flimsy fences string
together testament on
testament of rotted roses,
blackened dreams
& buried lives.

A woman in a hat too warm for the
weather climbs the ridgepole of a
sawhorse to get a better angle for her
snapshot. The policeman waves her
down just as she aims
& shoots.

Teenagers hand out felt-tip pens
to sign the flimsy scrims that go up
hourly. Someday, a whole, fantastical
tent may be constructed from their
cursive palimpsests
& arabesques.

St. Paul's Chapel is still a hospice.

In Trinity, poinsettias bloody the aisles.

Outside, the tombstones have been vacuumed.

The heaven's a baby blue,
deceptively mild
& much emptier.

Tiny, Odd Museums

They're in most towns,
Receptacles for memories
Nobody remembers
In sepia photos, faded ink.

Receptacles for memories,
Blinds drawn, heat off,
In sepia photos, faded ink,
The past's alive with ghosts.

Blinds drawn, heat off,
Nobody remembers.
The past's alive with ghosts.
They're in most towns.

Elegy in Five Parts

Tish #1. Solution

The catastrophic conduit
put in courtesy of the city
to channel the water
out to sea seems at least
a little less obtrusive
now that the heavy
equipment's gone,
not to mention the aqua
plastic portable toilet.
Unlike other entities,
water merely bides its time,
protean, capable of
spreading out in
a thousand different veins,
determined to surface
in basements in the
drenching wretchedness
of limping March, sucking
the life out of the furnace,
sending shoes and canisters
bobbing up the stairwell,
trying to drown the cat.
Naturally, no words
can dilute the rising sense
of uneasiness, programmed
into the genes since the Ark,
at the sight of black water
slithering over the bent,
knuckled knees of the willows,
nothing limpid about it,

performing its muscular duty
as a trunk line for hidden
sinews of water.
If you squint, Tish,
that brick ditch in the lawn
could almost be an artifact,
Roman, a viaduct,
something classic.
I said, *almost.*

Tish #2. Last Seen

Tish sits in her kitchen
at the glass table, organizing
a pool of spilled change.
Six glass cylinders
hold beach pebbles and
paperwhites still in their
shiny gold onionskins.
On her porch, hairy begonias
still defend their turf in a
white box tacked to
the gray wooden railing.
For November, it's mild,
eerily so, after a sodden spring,
sullen summer and terrifying fall.

I never dreamed anything
could be more bitter than February,
when I buried my mother
on a New Hampshire hillside
 so wind-whipped the tears

froze on my numb face.
That was back when Tish
could still afford to employ me
as dogsbody in the rarified trade
of Chinese objets d'art.

Every ornament in this place
had its price and the sticker
to prove it. But in these days
right after 9/11, no one's looking
for Jesuit-inspired ivory triptychs,
harbors painted backward
on glass, heavy silver tea sets
with faux English hallmarks
and teakwood handles,
a cockerel-crested thumb ring,
a card case carved of bone,
or a silk chasuble
the color and weight of dust.
Her robe is either a legitimate caftan
or an old bedspread. It could be
a remnant of the poor marriage
or the rich one, art school or just
the Sixties. In any event,
she's watching me unpack
the single grocery bag, smoking
a thirty-cent cigarette from
the pack I've just bought her,
and coughing. Blood mottles
the visible skin of her arms.
After two worming probes

at her heart in middle age, she's
self-employed and uninsured
so traded occidental medicine
for oriental herbs. They simmer
aromatically in an enameled
orange pot licked by
blue and gold tongues
from one of two burners still firing.
"What do I owe you," she says
from behind the squat fortress
of quarters she's stacked up
in a hard silver line on the table.
"My treat."
I put the dozen
ice cream cups, vanilla veined
with strawberry, or chocolate,
into the freezer along with
some lo-cal dinners.

Ginger ale goes below,
and the milk. I had bought
food like this for my mother,
trying to mend the growing gaps
in an ailing life with bricks
of frozen peas and colder mortar
of advice: "Heat up the soup,
make yourself some tea,
then take a nap."
Like my mother, she's hungry
for more than I've brought.
My mother paid January's bills,
balancing her checkbook on a tray
pushed up to her wheelchair.

When I pulled on my coat,
she made a face and then laughed,
asking, "Can't we find
more paperwork to do?"
But I had gone down
the nursing home hallway,
turning, turning, to wave.

Now Tish laughs.
"I don't want you to go.
I'm lonely."
With her duckling tufts of hair,
she looks and sounds
like a little girl fighting
a fear of the dark,
half afraid you'll believe her.
Not knowing that in four days
somebody else will find her
halfway down the staircase
in a blizzard of bills,
 her neck snapped as neatly
as a porcelain doll's,
I laugh, too.

Tish #3. I Wanted to Share

Here are some things
I did for you:
I planted an avocado pit,
then two.

I bought new placemats,
napkins, too,
looked up how to
make a *roux*.

I bought new curtains,
scrubbed the floor.
What do you think
I did that for?

I'd found a friend
who lived nearby.
I thought I'd call you,
by and by.

I planned for you
in many ways,
not knowing there'd be
no more days.

Tish #4. Elegy

I see you
in your sea-green
suit of
leggings
sweater
tiny string of
pearls
you lifted those
pearls to
your lips

when you were
being
self-conscious
you had eyes
like water
pale as water
water at the bottom
of a jade cup

Tish #5. Holiday Poem

Your paper-whites
are long, tall sallies,
necessarily
narcissistic,
but never
dim bulbs.

They are accomplished
comediennes,
jocund with
rapier wit.

They suck water.

They don't eat dirt.

They fire like pistols,
like pistons,
nowhere one minute,
gone the next.

They listen to the carols
like Moslems would a
mullah,
high on the fragile towers of
their glass-green necks.

Fire didn't take you out,
nor fear.
You took a trip.
You took a fall.

You're never coming back.

At all.

Key

No matter how old,
or unfamiliar,
or rusted, or misshapen,
or whatever else can be
the matter with a key,
just to throw it out,
into the trash with
the cabbage leaves
and waxy cartons, seems,
even more than wanton,
downright dangerous.

What if the new lock
suddenly seizes up?
What if the old door
despises the new lock
and rejects its stepchild,
the new key?
What if the person
who once owned this key
came back from the dead,
and wanted in?

Don't you think
you should take
this old key and put it
in a safe place, a place
thieves wouldn't think
to look, high up,
for instance,
I know, in a shoe,
an old shoe, which you've

92

tied to another old shoe
and slung up
over the telephone
wire so one dangles
into the other?

Whatever you do,
don't put it beneath
the mat or over the sill
or on the steps under a pot
filled with pebbles and dirt.
Such a position gives the key
credence and leads to the
falsest of hopes.

Baggage

Half unhinged,
old suitcase jaws,
"Take me where
you want to go,"
as if a puckered
pocket hid a map
to the site of
lost faces, of
loved hands on
this very handle,
shins banged from
desire, walking fast,
joy swung between.
Crumpled ribbons
lie slack, memories
unfolded, nothing
left to pack
for one last trip
to the curb.

Still, Life

What is a compendium, anyway?
It sounds Edwardian, heavy, thick, ornate,
something that would have the dust fly out of it
if you were crazy enough to thumb through.

We don't want to talk about dust, though, or ashes.

So, let's talk about granite, marble, mica,
how the crabgrass grows tougher by the year,
rooted in a firm belief it is precious.

God says we're all blades to the sickle.
When you're the one swinging it, everything's
a weed, going to seed in a hand-basket.

No, that's hell.

Oh, well...

If what we had wasn't heaven on earth,
it was pretty damned close.

About the Author

Born in Manchester, New Hampshire to Ukrainian parents, Nancy Brewka-Clark began her writing career at a daily newspaper chain on Boston's North Shore. Since she believes poetry is akin to magic and may come and go as the muse pleases, she also writes short stories, nonfiction, and plays that have been published by Adams Media, Three Rivers Press, Southeast Missouri State University Press, FunDead Publications of Salem, Smith and Kraus, YouthPLAYS of Los Angeles and Routledge, among others. A number of her flash comedies have been produced by the Gi60 International One-Minute Play Festival at Brooklyn College's New Workshop Theater and appear on YouTube along with a Play of the Month for NYC Playwrights.

For three decades Nancy also painted professionally under the name of Nascha, the nickname her father bestowed on her, creating unique gilt bas reliefs that combined 18th century New England colonial japanning and Ukrainian folk motifs. Her work was featured in *Yankee Magazine, The Boston Globe, The New York Times* and a host of other publications and was sold in museum shops, galleries and craft fairs where she made steadfast friends.

A lifetime devotee of Nathaniel Hawthorne, or more specifically, his enigmatic older sister Elizabeth, she lives in Beverly, Massachusetts, the home of 19th-century poet Lucy Larcom. Like Lucy, Nancy was the editor of the Wheaton College literary magazine *Rushlight,* their tenure being a century apart.

Kelsay Books

Made in the USA
Coppell, TX
06 January 2023

10587276R10059